Werewolves

Aaron Frisch

CREATIVE EDUCATION

Published by Creative Education
P.O. Box 227, Mankato, Minnesota 56002
Creative Education is an imprint of
The Creative Company
www.thecreativecompany.us

Design and production by
Christine Vanderbeek
Art direction by Rita Marshall
Printed in the United States of America

Photographs by Alamy (AF archive,
Ivy Close Images, Lordprice Collection,
Photos 12, Pictorial Press Ltd), Getty
Images (Fuse), Shutterstock
(Dreamframer, Mikhail, Sergey
Mironov, Neirfy, Photosani, Carolina
K. Smith, M.D.)

Library of Congress
Cataloging-in-Publication Data
Frisch, Aaron.
Werewolves / Aaron Frisch.
p. cm. — (That's spooky!)
Includes bibliographical references and
index.
Summary: A basic but fun exploration of
werewolves—shape-shifting monsters
with wolf features—including how they
come to exist, their weaknesses, and
memorable examples from pop culture.
ISBN 978-1-60818-249-7
1. Werewolves—Juvenile literature.
I. Title.

GR830.W4F75 2013
398.24'54—dc23   2011051181

9 8 7 6 5 4 3 2

CONTENTS

Imagine ... **4**

What Is a Werewolf? **7**

Becoming a Werewolf **8**

Werewolf Behavior **11**

A Werewolf's Powers **12**

A Werewolf's Weaknesses **15**

Famous Werewolves **16**

Give a Howl **20**

Learn to Spot a Werewolf **22**

Dictionary **23**

Read More **24**

Web Sites **24**

Index **24**

IMAGINE ...

You are walking through a forest at night. The moon is full. You hear a spooky howl. Then you hear something growl. Suddenly, a hairy beast jumps out. It's part man, part animal.

IT'S A WEREWOLF!

WHAT IS A WEREWOLF?

A werewolf is a man who turns into a wolf. In many cases, a werewolf does not look like a normal wolf. A werewolf might run on four legs or two legs. It has a long **SNOUT** and sharp teeth.

A wolf is like a big wild dog, only scarier

Becoming a Werewolf

A bite or scratch from a werewolf can turn a person into a werewolf. A **CURSE** might make a man a werewolf, too. Usually, a werewolf stays a normal person. But on nights when the moon is full, he turns into a beast!

People have always been afraid of wolves

WEREWOLF BEHAVIOR

When the moon turns a man into a werewolf, he becomes dangerous. A werewolf is very **AGGRESSIVE**. It might attack even its own friends and family.

The light of the moon drives a werewolf crazy

A WEREWOLF'S POWERS

It can be hard to figure out which people are werewolves. Werewolves are strong and can run fast. They have **SUPERHUMAN** senses of smell and hearing, too.

It is very hard to outrun a hungry werewolf

A Werewolf's Weaknesses

Werewolves are dangerous only during a full moon. When morning comes after a full moon, they change back into people. The only sure way to stop a werewolf is to shoot it with a silver bullet!

Werewolves do a lot of fighting and biting

FAMOUS WEREWOLVES

The Wolf Man is one of the most famous werewolves. He is the star of an old movie called *The Wolf Man*. He looks more like a very hairy man than a wolf.

The movie *The Wolf Man* came out in 1941

The WOLF MAN

with

CLAUDE RAINS
WARREN WILLIAM

Teen Wolf is a movie about a teenage werewolf. He uses his werewolf powers to become a great high-school basketball player. In the *Twilight* books and movies, some young men can turn into werewolves anytime they want!

Teen Wolf (above) and *Twilight* werewolves (left)

GIVE A HOWL

Werewolves are not real. They exist only in spooky stories. But pretending to be a werewolf can be fun. Find a furry outfit and some pointy fake teeth, then try out your best howl. Just stay away from silver!

A mask is the easiest way to turn into a wolf

long snout

sharp teeth

claws

fur

THAT'S SPOOKY!

LEARN TO SPOT A WEREWOLF

DICTIONARY

AGGRESSIVE acting in a mean way or wanting to fight

CURSE a kind of magic spell that does something bad to a person

SNOUT the long nose and mouth of some animals, such as dogs and wolves

SUPERHUMAN having powers or skills that are greater than a human being's

THAT'S SPOOKY!

WEREWOLVES

READ MORE

Hamilton, S. L. *Werewolves*. Edina, Minn.: Abdo, 2011.

Pipe, Jim. *Werewolves*. New York: Bearport, 2007.

Sautter, Aaron. *Werewolves*. Mankato, Minn.: Capstone, 2007.

WEB SITES

ACTIVITY TV: WEREWOLF COSTUME

http://www.activitytv.com/345-werewolf-costume

This video shows you how to make a quick werewolf costume.

FUNSCHOOL: HALLOWEEN

http://funschool.kaboose.com/fun-blaster/halloween/

This site has a lot of spooky games and pictures for coloring.

INDEX

becoming a werewolf **8**

curses **8**

full moons **4, 8, 11, 15**

howling **4, 20**

movies **16, 19**

senses **12**

silver bullets **15**

stopping a werewolf **15**

stories **19, 20**

teeth **7, 20, 22**

The Wolf Man **16**